LOOKS GOOD ON PAPER

an entr~   s guide

First edition

LOOKS GOOD ON PAPER

an entrepreneur's guide

BY

Jonathan Yates

Published by BOBYSHARK publishing

Copyright © 2008 by Jonathan Yates.

Published by BOBYSHARK publishing.

The rights of Jonathan Yates to be identified as the author of the work has been asserted by him in accordance with the Copyright, Designs & Patents Act, 1988. All rights reserved. No part of the publication may be reproduced, stored in a retrieval system, or transmitted, in any form or by any means without prior written permission of the publisher, nor be otherwise circulated in any form of binding or cover other than that in which it is published and without a similar condition being imposed on the subsequent purchaser.

A catalogue record for this title is available from the British Library.

ISBN 978-0-9559072-0-3

First Edition Printed and bound by BOOKPRINTINGUK.COM

ABOUT THE AUTHOR

Jonathan Yates is a serial entrepreneur, adventurer and sportsman appearing in the national press on many occasions and having his top tips for business success compared to those of business mogul and chairman of TV show The Apprentice, Sir Alan Sugar.

Businessman and Dragon's Den stalwart Peter Jones, impressed by Jon's business sense, In the Sunday Times, praised Jon for his entrepreneurialism and instinct, saying "it won't be long before he gets a loyal following."

Mike Clare, Founder of Dream Beds Plc. "Jonathan is one of those rare individuals who has great business acumen as well as entrepreneurial insight. His passion to succeed is infectious."

"Jon is quite simply the most motivated, single minded and self believing entrepreneur I have ever met. He will never accept that his goal is unreachable." Greg Smallwood, Investor.

ACKNOWLEDGEMENTS

My business is just getting going. I founded and sold my first company to help people drink more water and still work with this business every single day. I believe this insiders view gives recognition to the hardships and success involved in taking ideas forward in our current economic climate.

I am at the start of my entrepreneurial career and as such use the ideas in this book to help progress my own plans. I would not have completed the book without employing its wisdom.

The most valuable piece of advice that I turn to in times of trouble is *"Keep on going".* Thank you John Handley for unwavering support.

Thank you to all who have helped me in my various endeavors. It would have been impossible without you.

Jonathan Yates, Harrogate, 2008

HOW TO USE THIS BOOK

LOOKS GOOD ON PAPER has been created with the understanding that entrepreneurs like to find new and valuable ideas quickly. Read the information when you have a spare moment, when your head is clear and when you are receptive to innovative thinking.

Relax and embrace a single page, think about what that particular concept means and how it relates to you and your business ideas. Be open to changing perceptions to increase likelihood of success. This is a manual of ideas not an instruction booklet. It is up to you to interpret the meaning in this book and draw through your experiences to put into practice new strategies for success.

If you have questions or ideas you wish to explore then please email me at ***jon@jonathanyates.biz*** I am always excited to hear from people willing to take a next step.

LOOKS GOOD ON PAPER

an entrepreneur's guide

BY

Jonathan Yates

START

"Whatever you do, or dream you can do begin it. Boldness has genius, power, magic in it, begin it now."

Goethe

ONE (1)

Begin it now.

Take your idea, the one that has been running around your head, the one you have been telling you friends about and do something, anything to get it started. Write a description, sketch a prototype, search for similar products online or just pick up the phone and call someone.

The more you do the more real it becomes. If you talk and act like an entrepreneur, this is what you become.

"Work grows out of other work, and there are very few eureka moments."

Anish Kapoor

T W O (2)

The eureka moment.

The much talked about *eureka moment* is not a moment at all; it's a length of time that begins with learning and experiences which can be drawn on to realise logical conclusions.

The word Eureka means "I have found it". In order to find something you need to be looking for it in the first place. Go and look for your eureka moment.

"The best reason to start an organization is to make meaning - to create a product or service to make the world a better place."

Guy Kawasaki

THREE (3)

Start for a reason.

When you put your heart into a venture, real emotion, the process becomes all the more powerful.

Try holding back someone dedicated to a cause. They have an unstoppable attitude that far outstrips the need for financial gain.

Innovate with passion and the financial rewards will come.

"Traditional thinking is all about "what is." Future thinking will also need to be about what can be."

Edward de Bono

FOUR (4)

Learn to sell concepts.

The ability to sell an intangible idea is a necessary skill for innovators. You may have ideas that are not yet commercially available. When you are given the opportunity to sell in front of a buyer or investor then sell the concept, there may not be another chance.

Selling is always easier when you have something to show like a prototype or a client referral or even your research into the innovation, you have made it seem real for the buyer.

"Some people dream of great accomplishments, while others stay awake and do them."

Anon

FIVE(5)

Use your time wisely.

Time management is a mislabeled skill. What you need to manage is your activity during time. define outcomes and physical actions as the core process required to manage what you do.

An easy tool for activity management is prioritising. Ensure you are making the best use of your time right now by doing those things that grow the opportunity.

"I work with wonderful people who support me. And, my beliefs are that the business needs to serve the family rather than the family serve the business."

Kathy Ireland

SIX (6)

Involve family and friends.

In the startup phase your family and friends will be your closest advocates. Be warned, family and friends are not always the best people to approach for views on your business idea, they really want to be on your side and this may cloud judgement. Look to them for financial and emotional support but remember to listen to their advice objectively.

"We can never be certain about the future and therefore we must continue to be flexible and adaptable so that we can react quickly to the needs of our clients and our market place."

Talal Abu-Ghazaleh

SEVEN(7)

Smaller businesses are more agile.

Implement change quickly to take advantage of new opportunities. Large organisations have lengthy sign off procedures when innovating. You can make those decisions right now ahead of the competition.

Companies wait to see how a market takes off rather than produce an early start innovation and will look to purchase startups to get a foothold in a newly created market rather than risk starting from scratch.

"All people are entrepreneurs, but many don't have the opportunity to find that out."

Muhammad Yunus

EIGHT(8)

Step out of your career.

A career may seem safe. A steady, measured income with an expected salary each month is a comfortable place to be.

Are you happy making money for other people? Could you take your existing clients and start on your own? Are you ready to find out what life could be like? Ask yourself these questions and answer them honestly, it may be you are not ready for this massive leap of faith yet.

"A big part of financial freedom is having your heart and mind free from worry about the what-ifs of life."

Suze Orman

NINE (9)

Bootstrap financing.

Financial Bootstrapping is a term used to describe methods of self-financing for your project without the need for external investors. Many entrepreneurs turn to credit cards to help them launch the business to manage cash flow during startup. Another method is to stay in your current job until your business is ready to launch.

There are some very successful companies founded on the bootstrapping ethic, DELL computers is just one.

"Twenty years from now you will be more disappointed by the things that you didn't do than by the ones you did do. So throw off the bowlines. Sail away from the safe harbor. Catch the trade winds in your sails. Explore. Dream. Discover"

Mark Twain

TEN (10)

I always wanted to but...

It can only be up to one person to make this life changing decision. You need faith in your abilities and differentiation of product for the market. With hard work, tenacity and a little luck you have the chance to forge your own future.

What could be more satisfying than being in charge of your own destiny?

IDEAS

"Keep on going and the chances are you will stumble on something, perhaps when you are least expecting it. I have never heard of anyone stumbling on something sitting down."

Charles Kettering

ELEVEN(11)

You are unique.

The collection of diverse events you have experienced during your lifetime are unique to you and only you.

Use these experiences and connections to find insights and opportunities that no one else has the eyes to see.

You are unique. You will never, ever meet anyone like you. This is your competitive advantage.

"Opportunity is missed by most people because it is dressed in overalls and looks like work."

Thomas Edison

TWELVE (12)

Opportunities are everywhere.

Look at what annoys or upsets people; these are sources of opportunity.

The washer would not have been invented if it were not for the dripping tap. Everything we see around us has been invented for a reason - look at products and ask yourself what problem do they solve. Before long you will be seeing the problems that need solutions.

"We have two ears and one mouth so that we can listen twice as much as we speak."

Epictetus

THIRTEEN (13)

Listen to your customers.

Let your customers talk so you can learn their needs and determine how your products and services should best be tailored to solve their specific problems.

"My advice is never to set out just to be rich. Do what you love to do and if in the process you become rich then regard it as a bonus."

James Dyson

FOURTEEN (14)

Do something you enjoy.

You have interests and pastimes that you enjoy in your spare time. Group them together and see if there is a way to turn what you love doing into a business.

When you enjoy what you do every day will it feel like work?

"Watch, listen, and learn. You can't know it all yourself.. anyone who thinks they do is destined for mediocrity."

Donald Trump

FIFTEEN (15)

Learn a new skill.

You will have excellent skills yet to be discovered. Without trying something new you may never find out what could be the root of future success. There may be a relevant skill needed to plug a gap in the business but once in a while be interested in something you would never normally give time too. Embrace new things away from your day-to-day routines, try a new sport, buy a magazine, go on a course or volunteer to help in a friends business for a day.

Try new and different experiences and grow opportunities.

"If I have seen a little further it is by standing on the shoulders of Giants."

Descartes

SIXTEEN (16)

Take a brilliant idea and do it better.

Opportunity can often be found in existing products. Airlines such as Easyjet took the industry by storm, offering no frills air travel. Not radically different to the current offering but cheaper, opening up airtravel to the mass market. The changes you make do not have to be complicated, in fact the simpler, the better.

Use the advances in technology that others have created to move ahead a little further with your own ideas.

"Imagination is more important than knowledge. For knowledge is limited, whereas imagination embraces the entire world, stimulating progress, giving birth to evolution."

Albert Einstein

SEVENTEEN (17)

Harness the power of Imagination.

Notice how children's minds work, they are not constrained. Listen to the stories they make up and the make believe games they enjoy, where do these ideas come from?

Creativity is stifled during our working lives especially in corporate environments. Develop your own creativity by reading, drawing, singing and playing games. If you exercise creativity then it will be ready to work for you when you need it.

"Making money is a hobby that will complement any other hobbies you have, beautifully."

Scott Alexander

EIGHTEEN (18)

Appreciate other people's interests.

Every pastime is interesting to someone for a reason; find out what that reason is and see if it can be a benefit to your business. If you are unsure about this statement then research a seemingly uninteresting subject right now by purchasing a magazine on an obscure topic.

Opportunities are everywhere if you look carefully enough.

"Imitation is the sincerest form of flattery."

Charles Caleb Colton

NINETEEN (19)

Protect your ideas.

Your ideas are yours alone and need to be protected as soon as possible. Ideas are worth money. Contact local patent and trademark representatives to learn how to protect yourself from imitation.

The simplest way to protect your ideas is not to tell anyone unless they have signed a non-disclosure agreement [NDA]. Find a standard NDA on the Internet and tailor it to your needs.

"For a dream to become reality, make it real enough to believe in."

Peter Jones

TWENTY (20)

Create an elevator pitch.

Can you clearly and concisely convey your business idea in 10 seconds?

A good elevator pitch is a set of short statements covering who you are, what you do, and how your goods and services can offer value to customers.

Keep your pitch simple, understandable and concise.

MOTIVATION

"The reasonable man adapts himself to the world. The unreasonable man persists in trying to adapt the world to himself. Therefore, all progress depends on the unreasonable man."

George Bernard Shaw

T W E N T Y O N E (2 1)

Change is your responsibility.

Many people resist change and are comfortable with the way things are. Imagine what the world might be like if all the people with brilliant ideas did something with them instead of just talking about them.

"The way to get started is to quit talking and begin doing."

Walt Disney

TWENTYTWO (22)

Do it better.

Always ask yourself, whenever you are applauding a person, a product, a service, an idea or an achievement, "Could I have done that, Could I do it better?"

If the answer is yes then go and do it.

"The critical ingredient is getting off your butt and doing something. It's as simple as that. A lot of people have ideas, but there are few who decide to do something about them now. Not tomorrow. Not next week. But today. The true entrepreneur is a doer, not a dreamer"

Nolan Bushnell

TWENTYTHREE (23)

Don't just dream you can do it.

Sitting and talking is all well and good but you need to get out there and do the hard work. This is the part that most people misunderstand. It is the detail that needs to be progressed in order to make something real. It is easy to find a reason not to action something. Make the hard choice and decide to do it.

"The future you see is the future you get."

Robert Allen

TWENTYTFOUR(24)

Goal Setting.

Create a collection of pictures and cuttings that you can refer to when embracing your aspirations. Set them up in your office or on your fridge to remind you of grand plans. There might be a picture of a car, a description of a holiday destination or a deal with a particular client. Always visualize targets specific to your own personal aspirations.

What do you want in life? If you can see where you want to get to, you can plan the best route to get there.

"Every day, you'll have opportunities to take chances and to work outside your safety net. Sure, it's a lot easier to stay in your comfort zone... in my case, business suits and real estate.. but sometimes you have to take risks. When the risks pay off, that's when you reap the biggest rewards."

Donald Trump

TWENTYTFIVE(25)

Enjoy feeling uncomfortable.

We are comfortable with those experiences we are familiar with or have interest in. Introduce something new and we feel vulnerable and unable to control the situation.

It is vital that you embrace this feeling. Finding coping strategies with the unfamiliar are exactly what an entrepreneur thrives upon.

"Losers visualize the penalties of failure. Winners visualize the rewards of success."

Unknown

TWENTYSIX (26)

Visualise achievements.

Visualisation helps us to place ourselves in unfamiliar circumstances in advance. When the time comes for us to perform, we then find ourselves some way to being prepared.

You may be presenting an idea to a forum or winning a business deal but if you only visualise the goal then you have not realised the possible beneficial outcome. Always visualise successful achievements and make them happen.

"I felt a strange calmness… a kind of euphoria. I felt I could run all day without tiring, that I could dribble through any of their team or all of them, that I could almost pass through them physically."

Pelé

TWENTYSEVEN(27)

Embrace Flow.

Time seems to drag when we endure a difficult or tiresome task. When we enjoy ourselves time speeds up and the event is over too soon. Flow is a mental state in which a person is fully immersed in the task at hand, often characterised by a feeling of energised focus, full involvement, and success in the process of the activity.

Capture flow in all your endeavors and you have the mental aptitude for success.

"Along with a strong belief in your own inner voice, you also need laser-like focus combined with unwavering determination."

Larry Flynt

TWENTYEIGHT (28)

Keep on going.

There will be times when you want to give up; it's only natural as we have an in built fear of failure. You have come this far now and you have to see it through.

Go back to the issue that seems insurmountable and turn it on its head. Often in times of difficulty a stunning solution will present itself.

"Genius is 1% inspiration and 99% perspiration. Accordingly a genius is often merely a talented person who has done all of his or her homework."

Thomas Edison

TWENTYNINE(29)

If it was easy, everyone would do it.

Starting a successful business is hard with failures all too common. The journey requires emotion, commitment tenacity and dedicated work.

Starting a business is likened to riding a roller coaster with deep dark troughs and massive elative peaks.

Be prepared for both joys and disappointments.

"Motivation is a fire from within. If someone else tries to light that fire under you, chances are it will burn very briefly."

Stephen Covey

THIRTY (30)

Motivation by reward.

Motivation is behavior that you can influence but not create. Even highly motivated individuals get frustrated, discouraged, or tired.

Everyone needs to know their efforts are noticed, and their good work is appreciated. You are different and are motivated and rewarded by different things. Find out what these motivations are and use them to achieve your just rewards.

OPPORTUNITY

"The entrepreneur is our visionary, the creator in each of us. We're born with that quality and it defines our lives as we respond to what we see, hear, feel, and experience. It is developed, nurtured, and given space to flourish or is squelched, thwarted, without air or stimulation, and dies."

Michael Gerber

THIRTYONE (31)

Find out who you are.

- ***ALTREPRENEURS*** look for a change of lifestyle and not just increased wealth.

- ***ENTREPRENEURS*** make money out of ever changing market opportunities.

- ***ULTRAPRENEURS*** or serial entrepreneurs actively reinvest their money into ever larger business ventures.

"We are what we repeatedly do. Excellence, therefore, is not an act but a habit."

Aristotle

THIRTYTWO (32)

Do the research.

You have the idea now test the market. Conduct face-to-face interviews using tailored questionnaires directly with your target audience. There are many free online services, which can help you do this. You may already have an email list of friends and family; ask them relevant questions. Trawl the Internet; there is a universe of information which can help your proposition become real for investors, customers and suppliers.

Prove the idea is real.

"It isn't just what you know, and it isn't just who you know. It's actually who you know, who knows you, and what you do for a living."

Bob Burg

THIRTYTHREE (33)

Grow your personal network.

Attend free seminars and business functions to meet people from outside your industry. You may find future clients and more effective suppliers.

Local business organisations are looking to grow their network by asking people like you to attend.

You have the opportunity to spend every morning and every evening networking so pick and choose those to suit you needs.

"The world is more malleable than you think and it's waiting for you to hammer it into shape."

Bono

THIRTYFOUR (34)
Take every opportunity.

If someone asks your advice when looking to purchase a product or service, be bold and say "Yes, that is something we can deliver for you." Then go away and find a way to do it.

Do it well to ensure repeat business and unprompted referrals.

"When I started out in business, I spent a great deal of time researching every detail that might be pertinent to the deal I was interested in making. I still do the same today. People often comment on how quickly I operate, but the reason I can move quickly is that I've done the background work first, which no one usually sees."

Donald Trump

THIRTYFIVE (35)

Simple Research: read a magazine.

Research is fundamental to the success of your burgeoning idea so read a magazine as a very easy first step. Each industry has a trade magazine full of qualified and experienced writers. Do your research and educate yourself about the industry to become an expert.

Your customers and competitors are reading the same material so use this newfound knowledge to gain insight, ideas and sales leads.

"Conformity is the jailer of freedom and the enemy of growth."

John F. Kennedy

THIRTY SIX (36)

Scalability.

If you have seen the opportunity to do something better then create the solution but remember a very important rule: Create a solution that everyone needs and not a product that solves a problem for you alone. You may have created a product with only one satisfied customer.

Ensure your product or service can be produced and sold in quantity to satisfy a larger market opportunity and to enjoy better commercial terms by increasing production run orders.

"Whether you think you can or think you can't, you're right."

Henry Ford

THIRTYSEVEN(37)

Be tenacious.

Tenacity: To hold persistently to something, such as a point of view.

You are right! Which is exactly why you started the company in the first place. Ensure that you are doing everything necessary to show your unshakeable point of view backed up by evangelical zeal.

" The fact is, everyone is in sales. Whatever area you work in, you do have clients and you do need to sell."

Jay Abraham

THIRTYEIGHT (38)

Listen and understand.

When selling a product or service, listen to the client's issues to understand their requirements. The customer will already have an idea of what they want to buy.

Understand requirements first before telling them all about what you can do for them; it may just miss their expectations. Tailor your sales pitch to customer specific needs and you will have created a specific solution that your client will be unable to replicate.

"I have yet to find the man, however exalted his station, who did not do better work and put forth greater effort under a spirit of approval than under a spirit of criticism."

Charles Schwab

THIRTYNINE (39)

Absorb criticism and use it.

There are often times when peers will criticise your ideas. Use this fantastic opportunity to question their thoughts. These ideas could be the foundations of a successful direction for your business. Accept help in all its forms.

"Even in such technical lines as engineering, about 15% of one's financial success is due to one's technical knowledge and about 85% is due to skill in human engineering, personality and the ability to lead people."

Dale Carnegie

FORTY (40)

Surround yourself with intelligence.

A good leader will hire employees who are more intelligent than they are.

An effective leader will understand that good employees will always have a better grasp of an area of expertise.

An entrepreneur should know a little about a wide range of subjects to draw on experience, the employee should be an expert in a single subject area.

CHALLENGES

"When you confront a problem you begin to solve it."

Rudy Giuliani

FORTYONE(41)

Embrace problems.

Don't stick your head in the sand, the issue will not go away on its own, you have to stand up and confront an issue in order to start solving it.

Ask for help.

"I wanted to be an editor or a journalist, I wasn't really interested in being an entrepreneur, but I soon found I had to become an entrepreneur in order to keep my magazine going."

Richard Branson

FORTYTWO(42)

When things get tough keep going.

Becoming an entrepreneur is inevitable when starting a new venture. You will have to overcome stumbling blocks by using entrepreneurial skills and attitudes to overcome seemingly insurmountable problems. There is always a way, you just need to find it.

"I have not failed. I've just found 10,000 ways that won't work."

Thomas Edison

FORTYTHREE (43)

Learn from mistakes.

We all make mistakes from time to time and will continue to do so. Make sure that you take a lesson from each failure and never repeat it. Build on success and learn from failures.

"A real entrepreneur is somebody who has no safety net underneath them."

Henry Kravis

FORTYFOUR (44)

Overcome big issues.

When a large issue raises its head, break it down into component parts to find a different route through.

Write down five things you need to do to get over the problem, then take each of these five solutions and write five ways to achieve them. You now have a solid action plan to follow to get round the problem.

"An entrepreneur tends to bite off a little more than he can chew hoping he'll quickly learn how to chew it"

Roy Ash

FORTY (45)

If you find it tough, that's good.

If things are easy when setting up your business, like finding a supplier for a new product innovation for example, then its probably been done before.

Sometimes the harder it is, the more likely it is to be true innovation and the harder you should push the opportunity to make it work.

"You can get everything in life you want if you will just help enough other people get what they want."

Zig Ziglar

FORTYSIX (46)

Ask for help.

When you have an issue with a complex aspect of your business why not contact a company you admire in a different industry and ask them how they do it. You will have widened your network and found out in an instant how to solve some of your current challenges.

"In any situation, the best thing you can do is the right thing; the next best thing you can do is the wrong thing; the worst thing you can do is nothing."

Theodore Roosevelt

FORTYSEVEN (47)

Make a list to manage time.

You can't manage time, it just is. What you really manage is your activity during time, and defining outcomes and physical actions required is the core process required to manage what you do every day.

Create a list and work through it. Those items that you don't do today put at the top of the list tomorrow. If items are on the list for more than a week then discard them, they will not get done.

"The Chinese use two brush strokes to write the word 'crisis'. One brush stroke stands for danger; the other for opportunity. In a crisis, be aware of the danger-but recognize the opportunity."

John F. Kennedy

FORTYEIGHT(48)

Crisis opportunity.

In times of crisis there will be opportunity. Be creative with your ideas when looking for a path to success.

Find it, seize it, use it, you are an entrepreneur and this is a rime full of opportunity.

"Sometimes the situation is only a problem because it is looked at in a certain way. Looked at in another way, the right course of action may be so obvious that the problem no longer exists."

Edward de Bono

FORTYNINE (49)

Walk around a problem.

There will always be a way through an issue, you just have to find that way. Confront the issue head on, from the sides and in every conceivable angle. Don't be afraid to take advice whatever the problem is, there may have been someone who has faced similar issues before.

"Insanity: doing the same thing over and over again and expecting different results."

Albert Einstein

FIFTY (50)

Learn to adapt, think creatively.

If a singular course of action is not returning the desired results, stop and try a new approach.

Do not panic, there will be a way around the problem. Be willing to try new things to adapt to a situation.

Think creatively.

MARKETING

" If you do build a great experience, customers tell each other about that. Word of mouth is very powerful."

Jeff Bezos

FIFTYONE(51)

Evangelise your services.

If you are unable to be excited about you services then how can you expect your customers to become excited and spread the word on your behalf.

Use your own products and services everyday. Eat, live and breathe your business.

Be your most critical customer.

"And I'm not an actress. I don't think I am an actress. I think I've created a brand and a business."

Pamela Anderson

FIFTYTWO (52)

Create a brand.

Brand your offering to gain a loyal customer base.

If you can answer the following two questions then you have a brand. What is your point? Why should anyone care? Take the answers to these two questions and create your brand identity around them.

A brand can be developed from any sized business in any industry.

"Attitudes are contagious. Make yours worth catching."

Unknown

FIFTYTHREE (53)

Create customer involvement.

Involve clients in your business. Aim to inform and educate and not simply to sell products and services. Actively involve customers in all aspects of your business, get them talking about it and keep them emotionally involved with regular two way communications in the form of newsletters, phone calls and personalised emails, competitions and questionnaires.

"The brand is a contractual promise between you and your customers. A logo is your signature on that contract."

Anonymous

FIFTYFOUR (54)

A Brand is a promise.

Customer loyalty is nurtured through the time and experience of clients dealing with your brand. If you can consistently deliver the ideals of the brand to the expectations of the client then they will consistently buy into your brand identity.

"The difference between ordinary and extraordinary is that little extra."

Unknown

FIFTY FIVE (55)

Break constraints.

If your idea is truly innovative then it may be difficult to persuade suppliers to work in a new way, especially if you are a small organisation or start up. Try not to be constrained by existing practices, push to get exactly what you want and the products you require to start your business and satisfy the market demand.

Compromise may mean the death of your innovation for the selected target audience.

"While it may be true that the best advertising is word-of-mouth, never lose sight of the fact it also can be the worst advertising."

Jef Richards

FIFTYSIX (56)

Create a buzz.

Word-of-mouth is a very powerful marketing tool that every entrepreneur must use. It can be low-cost, requires very little budget, and works when we sleep.

Talk to friends, Educate opinion leaders, Pitch a story to the media, Send an email newsletter, Run a competition or start a blog. Learn about the various viral marketing techniques and make them work for you.

"If we want a love message to be heard, it has got to be sent out. To keep a lamp burning, we have to keep putting oil in it."

Mother Teresa

FIFTYSEVEN (57)

Make yourself heard.

There is so much advertising noise in the world with thousands of confusing messages being shouted at us every day.

Don't just shout loudly to be heard, communicate cleverly with consistent messages to ensure you stand out from the competition and be heard above the background noise.

"A brand for a company is like a reputation for a person. You earn reputation by trying to do hard things well."

Jeff Bezos

FIFTYEIGHT (58)

Create a family of products.

If you have a successful product or service then alter the appeal for a different target market. Extending your range could be a simple and effective growth strategy.

Range extension may be as simple as re-packaging or repositioning the product to an alternative target audience or even to another industry.

Loyal customers will support you if you can offer relevant range extensions.

"Everything you do or say is public relations."

Anonymous

FIFTYNINE (59)
Create your own PR.

Every business needs publicity to spread the word, gain new business and build trust and credibility. You have the emotion in your business so use it to convey personal stories to the media. Editors like to hear real life stories from the founder of the business.

Prepare a press release, use free PR distribution web services and pick up the phone to newspapers and magazines that offer relevant editorial coverage for your customer base.

"It is not the strongest of the species that survive, nor the most intelligent, but the one most responsive to change."

Charles Darwin

SIXTY (60)

Be positively disruptive.

Create disruption in the field in which you want to be heard. Take a maverick approach and change the way people do business in your chosen industry. Xerox invented the computer mouse but did not promote the technology due to foreseen losses to its paper copying business. Apple, who had nothing to lose by pushing screen based technologies, launched a very successful computer company.

People resist change; you need to create it.

SALES

"Formula for success: under promise and over deliver"

Tom Peters

SIXTYONE(61)

Under promise and over deliver.

If you constantly exceed the expectations of your clients they have few reasons to look for your competitors.

Be careful not to set expectations too high as you must consistently deliver.

"No matter what your product is, you are ultimately in the education business. Your customers need to be constantly educated about the many advantages of doing business with you, trained to use your products more effectively, and taught how to make never-ending improvement in their lives."

Robert G Allen

SIXTYTWO (62)

Sell benefits not features.

Products and services are solutions to everyday problems.

Try to sell the features of tap water: A combination of Hydrogen and Oxygen in liquid state. Not very appealing. People may be put off by the technical words. If you say tap water is a refreshing, free soft drink that helps you rehydrate, quench your thirst and keeps you cool, you are solving problems. Put these two statements together to create your elevator pitch.

"Living on Earth may be expensive, but it includes an annual free trip around the sun."

Ashleigh Brilliant

SIXTYTHREE (63)

Generate goodwill.

Customers who receive an unexpected bonus whilst doing business will always remember you went further than competition.

Try a buy one get one free offer or take a client out to a smart restaurant. Arrange for your top 10 clients to meet up for a free networking seminar. Send insights into your customers industry. Do things that set you apart; your competitors may be doing the same so be creative.

"In sales, a referral is the key to the door of resistance."

Bo Bennett

SIXTYFOUR (64)

Ask for a referral.

Referrals begin with providing your current customers with prompt and reliable quality of service. They'll be happy to spread the word on your behalf, often without you having to ask.

When a customer compliments you on your work, ask them to put it in writing for use as a testimonial in your marketing materials.

"If it's free, it's advice; if you pay for it, it's counseling; if you can use either one, it's a miracle."

Jack Adams

SIXTYFIVE (65)

Provide free advice for customers.

Create a seminar that is informative to your client base. Use this forum to communicate the availability of new products and services they may not have seen or heard of before.

Ask one of your clients to be a keynote speaker on some element of your industry. They will feel honoured to help out.

"The best teamwork comes from men who are working independently toward one goal in unison."

James Cash Penney

SIXTYSIX (66)

Make yourself part of the team.

Demonstrate that you are there to help customers increase profits and solve business problems. Become indispensable and they will start to call you for advice rather than you calling them to sell.

The more integrated you are, the harder it will be for a competitor to move in so make your services and wisdom indispensable.

"Not being in tune with your customers is like living in an alternate reality; the way you think your customers feel about your product is not always the same as what your customers really think about your product."

Bo Bennett

SIXTYSEVEN (67)

Create excellent customer service.

Keep customers coming back by making sure your products or services work well for them. If problems persist, show concern and provide solutions at your own cost.

Goodwill is accountable and is reflected in the value of the business.

"A friendship founded on business is better than a business founded on friendship."

John Rockefeller

SIXTYEIGHT (68)

Don't have clients, have friends.

Be the preferred provider of information for your customers. Ensure they want to come to you for advice on a particular topic. Meet outside of the work environment and gain a personal rather than simply a business relationship.

"Business is not financial science, it's about trading.. buying and selling. It's about creating a product or service so good that people will pay for it."

Anita Roddick

SIXTYNINE (69)

Ask for the sale.

Many people are worried by the thought of selling. You have created a product that people will want to buy.

A sale is a two-way conversation. Talk to the prospect and answer the questions. When you have answered all the questions and the time is right then ask for the sale, the customer can only say no. You need ongoing sales to survive so if they persistently say no, waste no more time, move on and find a more committed client.

"Let us move from the era of confrontation to the era of negotiation."

Richard M. Nixon

SEVENTY (70)

Negotiation.

Buying and selling is trading. All trading is completed at a cost to those who want your product set at the price you would like them to pay. Negotiation enables fair-trading.

Be creative with your negotiation, don't make it just about price. You could offer a service contract or a monthly health check instead. Cash is king. Keep the price high to maximise cashflow and offer other items in negotiation that you can afford to give away.

STRATEGY

"Position yourself as a center of influence - the one who knows the movers and shakers. People will respond to that, and you'll soon become what you project."

Bob Burg

SEVENTYONE (71)
Become an expert.

Become an expert by writing impartial and informative articles on issues that affect your prospective customers. Offer them free of charge to newspapers and trade publications. Be sure to follow editorial guidelines and focus on providing helpful information instead of making a sales pitch.

"In preparing for battle I have always found that plans are useless, but planning is indispensable"

Dwight Eisenhower

SEVENTYTWO (72)

Things have a habit of snowballing.

Keep control of business focus by managing your plans. If things get out of control you will lose business momentum and end up firefighting instead of solving issues. This could very easily become time consuming and costly to your future success.

" Advertising is about norms and values, aspirations and prejudices. It is about culture."

Anil Ambani

SEVENTYTHREE (73)

Create a unique business culture.

You are your business, be comfortable with giving your emotion to the business and creating a culture of words, pictures and identity which customers and partners can tap into.

When you create a unique culture you create involvement for your stakeholders.

"I have always loved the competitive forces in this business. You know I certainly have meetings where I spur people on by saying, "Hey, we can do better than this. How come we are not out ahead on that?" Thats what keeps my job one of the most interesting in the world."

Bill Gates

SEVENTY FOUR (74)

Punch above your weight.

Compete at a level above your expectations to achieve greater rewards.

By placing yourself in circumstances that motivate you to work hard in order to gain control will move your business forward exponentially.

Position yourself with leading products and services to gain credibility by association.

"There are risks and costs to a program of action. But they are far less than the long-range risks and costs of comfortable inaction."

John F. Kennedy

SEVENTYFIVE (75)

De-risk the proposition.

To convince investors, suppliers and customers you must limit the risk you are asking people to take when investing time and money in you and your products.

Start by asking yourself if your goals are achievable. Once you have motivated yourself then you are prepared to de-risk the ideas for your family, the bank, suppliers, customers and consumers. De-risking is a business fundamental. People do not like to take risks its your task to convince them otherwise.

"Keep your friends close, and your enemies closer."

Sun-tzu

SEVENTYSIX (76)

Keep competitors close.

Get to know your competitors in a professional and personal capacity. They may need help with backlogs and overflow business, or with specialised services they are unable to offer.

This works the other way around when you offer a service for the first time and need to ask help from a competitor to get the business closed and retain a client. Knowing what your competitors are planning helps you organise for the future.

"Refusing to ask for help when you need it is refusing someone the chance to be helpful."

Ric Ocasek

SEVENTYSEVEN (77)

Outsource.

During the startup process you must do everything to make your business work. You will surprise yourself at the ease in which many new challenges are overcome. However, recognise the skills you lack and if need be then outsource to find complimentary expertise.

Stick to these three golden rules for best practice: Look for a business partner, not just a provider. Set and agree clear goals, objectives and expectations. Develop a business relationship based on mutual trust.

"Strangers are just friends who haven't yet met!"

Peter Rosen

SEVENTYEIGHT (78)

Call someone new right now.

Pick up the phone and call someone you respect in business or the community and introduce yourself and your products. Ensure your conversation is relevant and personalised and you will now have one of the following:

A new client, a new member of your personal network, some new information on the industry you work in or someone who can pass on your details to interested contacts.

"Doctors and scientists said that breaking the four-minute mile was impossible, that one would die in the attempt. Thus, when I got up from the track after collapsing at the finish line, I figured I was dead."

Roger Bannister

SEVENTYNINE (79)

Move the boundaries.

There will be times when suppliers say - "we don't do it like that." Ask them why, it may be they have never been asked before. You may be pulled down a route that satisfies a supplier's solution, by doing so they get your business. Try not be constrained, make sure you stick to your original product specification however hard it seems to do so at the time. The harder it is to create a new product or service means one of two things: Either there is no market need or you have true innovation.

"Rest when you're weary. Refresh and renew yourself, your body, your mind, your spirit. Then get back to work."

Ralph Marston

EIGHTY (80)

Take a day off.

Running a business is all consuming, take a day off away from email and switch off your phone. Take a break away and go for a walk or enjoy a sport. Learn something completely different with no perceived relevance to you business. It's healthy to be away from work for a while.

It is often in times of quite contemplation that we generate the best ideas.

MONEY

"Nobody talks of entrepreneurship as survival, but that's exactly what it is and what nurtures creative thinking."

Anita Roddick

EIGHTYONE (81)

Manage Cash flow.

Anyone can start a business but very few people can start a profitable business. The key to success during startup is cashflow survival; regular income enables you to grow the business at a realistic rate to achieve the business goals you set yourself.

"I never get the accountants in before I start up a business. It's done on gut feeling"

Richard Branson

E I G H T Y T W O (8 2)

Manage spending.

During startup when income is at its lowest, you will need to decide very carefully those products and services you spend your own money on. Look for alternatives in all aspects of business.

Use free online and open source office tools. Find free business card printing websites. Outsource until you can fund quality employees. Go the virtual route and work from home.

"Perhaps the very best question that you can memorize and repeat, over and over, is, what is the most valuable use of my time right now?"

Brian Tracy

EIGHTYTHREE (83)

Work on the business.

Your business may be running smoothly but take time to work on the development of the whole business and not just in the day-to-day work.

Using your time efficiently is the difference between busyness*{sic}* and effective business.

Work on the business and not just in the business.

"It has been my observation that most people get ahead during the time that others waste time."

Henry Ford

EIGHTYFOUR(84)

Lean how to organise.

Organise time, people, products, logistics, manufacturing, design and finance. If you can organise yourself then you are certainly able to organise a business.

We all have the ability to organize and make things happen so go ahead and do it.

"Repetition makes reputation and reputation makes customers."

Elizabeth Arden

EIGHTYFIVE (85)

Always ask for more.

Ensure suppliers are providing you with the best possible deal. Be creative when asking for something extra, allow your suppliers to show how valued you are and in return maintain your business with them.

Always compare at least three different suppliers by asking for written quotations and references. Make sure you follow up on the references to understand how other companies have benefited from their expertise.

"I think this is also a great time to invest in private equity, helping companies grow from the ground up."

Jim Rogers

EIGHTYSIX (86)

Use the equity you have.

In times of financial insecurity, use the equity built up as collateral in the business. First time entrepreneurs exit their first business with, on average, 7% of the company they founded.

Don't be precious with your first business, the key is to get it going and move it forward. If you have done it once then you can definitely do it again.

"Investors don't like uncertainty."

Kenneth Lay

EIGHTYSEVEN(87)

What do investors look for.

- Is there a market need for the product or service?

- Is the product or service commercially scalable?

- Do you have access to a good management team?

- Are you willing to risk your own finances?

  and most importantly

- Are you the right person to make it happen?

"Flying is learning how to throw yourself at the ground and miss."

Douglas Adams

EIGHTYEIGHT(88)

Try something completely different.

Expand your experiences buy trying something completely different outside your normal scope of comfort.

Join a group, try a sport, take a course, watch a film, try some new food, buy a different book, call a company you admire.

All of these activities will give you insights into other people's worlds and provide you with pathways to new opportunities.

"Business is other people's money."

Delphine de Girardin

EIGHTYNINE(89)

Use other people's money.

Be willing to give up a share in your company in order to start the business. Do not use all of your own finances just in case things go wrong. You may need a fall back.

There are hundreds of investment groups including Regional Investment firms, Business Angels and Government agencies. Approach some of these with a business plan to see if your idea is worth investing in.

At the very least it is another perspective on your idea.

"The whole is more than the sum of its parts."

Aristotle

NINETY (90)

Goodwill is accountable.

Everything you do in business and with your customers affects your reputation. Goodwill is an accounting term used to describe intrinsic value above the assets of the company that translate directly to the bottom line.

Do everything to maintain and grow Goodwill between you and your target audience in all its forms.

SUCCESS

"The only place where success comes before work is in the dictionary"

Vidal Sassoon

NINETYONE (91)

Hard work does pay off.

Ask your friends and colleagues if they enjoy their day-to-day job. Two thirds of the working population would rather be doing something else instead of their current work. How hard do you think these people are working?

Now find some self-employed entrepreneurs and ask them the same question. The answer will most likely be that the work is hard and the hours are long but the rewards are great and they enjoy going to work every single day.

"Some people fold after making one timid request. They quit too soon. Keep asking until you find the answers. In sales there are usually four or five "no's" before you get a "yes.""

Jack Canfield

N I N E T Y T W O (9 2)

When people say "NO!"

Find out why people are putting up barriers - The negativity may not always be founded on what you had expected.

Remember, in business it is much easier to say no. Be bold enough to ask the difficult questions and challenge the answers with creative reasoning.

"I've always worked very, very hard, and the harder I worked, the luckier I got."

Alan Bond

NINETYTHREE(93)

An element of luck.

However hard you work there will be times when things naturally fall into place with little effort. Luck and chance play important roles in your success.

We all know people who are naturally lucky. The ones who make things look easy are often those who work the hardest.

"A journey of a thousand miles starts with the first step."

Confucious

NINETYFOUR (94)

Enjoy small successes.

Small successes and little wins are the building blocks of large successes. Jump from win to win and grow in confidence.

Remember small triumphs when things look grey and how you went about achieving them to ensure you have enough confidence to overcome trivial issues.

"I never perfected an invention that I did not think about in terms of the service it might give others... I find out what the world needs, then I proceed to invent."

Thomas Edison

NINETYFIVE (95)

Create solutions to problems.

If you can solve a problem endured by millions then you have a product and a market.

Dyson saw the problem was changing hover bags, by doing away with the bag, Dyson had solved that problem. Simple.

Find out what frustrates people and see if there is an opportunity for you to do things better.

"Part of the issue of achievement is to be able to set realistic goals, but that's one of the hardest things to do because you don't always know exactly where you're going, and you shouldn't."

George Lucas

NINETY SIX (96)

Set realistic achievable goals.

Set goals over which you have as much control as possible. There is nothing more frustrating than failing to achieve a personal goal for reasons that are beyond your control. Be realistic and set small achievable goals to boost confidence with little but meaningful wins.

"Every worthwhile accomplishment, big or little, has its stages of drudgery and triumph; a beginning, a struggle and a victory"

Mahatma Gandhi

NINETYSEVEN (97)

There will be challenging times.

It is imperative that you regain focus for the task you have set yourself. There will be times when competitors out flank you or when nature conspires to disrupt your business. These are mostly outside of your control.

Learn from disasters and work them to your advantage. Where some people take an easy route back to their original lives you have to strive and persevere to succeed in the goals you are seeking to achieve.

"Being a top athlete requires total concentration. And some sacrifices. I have suffered a great deal, but here's the result. Never give up, make your dreams come true"

Alain Robert

NINETYEIGHT(98)

Perspective.

Emotion during the startup phase is a powerful ally but can confuse you in times of success and failure so remember:

It's never as good or as bad as it seems at the time.

"Entrepreneurship is living a few years of your life like most people won't, so that you can spend the rest of your life like most people can't."

Anon

NINETYNINE(99)

Do everything to make the idea real.

You have decided to start your adventure. This is an opportunity to create your own destiny. You will need to do everything and anything to make your business a success. Invest time, money and emotion. Live and breathe your product to ensure a successful conclusion.

"The greatest reward in becoming a millionaire is not the amount of money that you earn. It is the kind of person that you have to become to become a millionaire in the first place"

Jim Rohn

ONEHUNDRED(100)

It's not about the money.

What type of person do you need to be to achieve success? Are you a born innovator or do you need to learn the rudiments of entrepreneurship in order to get a first step ahead? Only you can answer these questions so make the journey about you.

When you act like an entrepreneur, by doing and saying those things to move your idea forward, people will look on you as an entrepreneur. An entrepreneur is something you become.